I0471063

How to sell your Christmas Crafts

Brenda Hunt

Marketing for Small Business Series

Introduction

So you want to sell Christmas Crafts.
What are Christmas crafts?
Or do you want to sell craft at Christmas?
What's the difference?
Well actually there is a difference.

Christmas crafts are pieces that will only work for the Christmas season - designs for the tree, Christmas crackers, Christmas wreaths, swags and other decorations.

But in fact almost any craft can be adapted to make the most of holiday sales.

If you decide to sell designs that will only find a market for the holiday season you will have to dedicate most of the year to designing and making, building up your stock and then find as many outlets as possible for the actual Christmas selling season – which begins late September, early October and can run right up until Christmas eve – depending on where you sell.

If you plan on selling your designs all year round but want to make the most of the holiday sales season, you also need to start planning much earlier than you might think.

Whichever way you plan on adapting your craft for Christmas, planning is an essential part of your plan – both in designing your actual products and in designing how you will package and display them to make the most of the vital Christmas sales season.

This book will guide you through the whole process - how to create your style, how to promote your business, how to layout your shopfront, how to decide on packaging and presentation.

It will also give you some ideas about where you can set up your shopfront. Craft fairs are the obvious first step, but Christmas is the time of most choice for selling opportunities for the crafter. There are specialist Christmas festivals and markets, school and church fairs, large Christmas craft markets and of course events in shopping malls.

Although there is always a lot of money spent during the holiday season, there is also a great deal of competition for it, so you need to be prepared and make the very most of the Christmas season.

What is Marketing and why is it important?

Although this book is about selling your Christmas crafts and selling your crafts at Christmas, you still need some basic information about the art of marketing.

Marketing is a vital skill no matter what you intend to sell how you plan on selling it. It will help you see your designs as a product, and more importantly as a product that other people will want to buy. That's the real difference between having a hobby and making items for yourself and friends, and having a business.

Why should you care about marketing?

So why am I starting with marketing?

It's because marketing is at the heart of any successful professional venture. In fact, this whole book is really about marketing and how you can use marketing to create your business and to grow to whichever level of business you want.

Some people will be happy to keep their craft business small, a home business that is focused on one person. Some will expand it to a family business selling on-line and through some craft shops as well as face to face, and others will want to create a brand that will be found in stores across the country.

But in this book we are focusing on the early stages of your new business and how to make the best of your opportunities when selling direct to your customer face-to-face.

What is marketing?

Many small businesses make the mistake of thinking that the whole concept of marketing is only something for big business.

That it's the world of the Marketing Director, huge budgets, huge departments, specialist agencies and the multi-national companies.

But at its heart, marketing is basic common sense.

Know what your customer wants - and supply it.

In fact, it's such basic common sense that some huge multi-national companies, with their huge marketing budgets and high powered marketing departments, completely lose sight of it, and then they lose sight of their customers as they leave in droves and go somewhere else that does still supply what they want.

Think of the mess some of the big high street names get themselves into when they decided that they know better than their customers. They start losing their customers - which for any company, means losing your business - and it can take them years and a huge amount of work to get them back.

Another misconception is that Sales and Marketing are the same thing - but they're not.

A Sales Campaign - selling your idea to the public and persuading them that they can't live without your product, can be a very expensive process. TV adverts, billboards, newspaper & magazine advertising are well out of reach for a small business. The world of the Internet and social media has opened it up if you are savvy with the technology, but it still doesn't get you the huge coverage and it still isn't the same as marketing. Companies can and have, spent huge amounts of money on trying to sell a product but failed at the end of the day because they've failed on the basic principle of marketing - they're trying to sell something that people don't want!

So, although some things may be out of the reach of the small business, really good marketing is something that the smallest of start up business can - indeed have to be - really good at.

After all, if you can't afford an expensive TV advertising campaign you'd better make sure that you're supplying exactly what your customer is looking for!

Market research

Every successful business knows who their target audience is. Look around at shops, magazines, fashion companies, car companies, holiday companies and designs companies.

Take one area of business and really look at them in detail rather than just at the ones that you normally buy from.

For instance spend a day at your nearest large shopping mall and study the stores that sell clothes - you need to visit a large shopping mall so that you have a full range of outlets to study.

You may never have really thought about it, but you'll know which ones attract you personally and which ones you'd never think of shopping in. But what is it about the brands and their shops that give you these signals?

This time really look at all of them, really study them.

Who do they target?

What age range?

What style?

What budget?

Decide what type of people would shop in that store.

What age, what life style, what career?

Where would they go for the evening? What type of holiday would they take? What type of car would they buy? And how can you tell that?

For this process, don't worry about being judgmental - you are trying to judge, you're learning how to judge what type of customer is going to want your designs!

Apart from the prices - which might not always be obvious straight away (in-fact the presence or absence of obvious prices can tell you something as well) - how can you tell the difference between the budget shop and the expensive?

What is the difference in the shopping experience between the designer boutique and the outlet that sells quality classic pieces?

Look at the decor of the shops, the colours, the style of their furnishings, the way they use the space.

How do they display their stock? Is every inch of space used or do they display a smaller number of pieces, giving each individual outfit space to be seen? Do they sell a jacket or do they sell the whole outfit as a 'look'.

How do they package their product? You don't actually have to purchase anything, although that can be fun and is certainly a way of finding out how they treat their customers, how they make you feel about your purchase and the whole experience of dealing with the company.

But if you decide that the process of market research doesn't stretch to a £350 Mulberry purse (sad but true!) just find a coffee shop or seat close to the shop and watch customers come and go. Is their purchase just stuffed into a plastic bag or is it carefully wrapped in tissue paper and gently placed in a beautiful, branded bag with ribbon handles? Think of what you would prefer as a customer.

Times are tough at the moment and it seems that they are going to stay that way for a while yet, so parting with money should be a pleasure. The experience should be fun, enjoyable and memorable for the right reasons. After all, when you buy new clothes, chocolates, cosmetics or a piece of designs, it's a treat, no matter how much or little you're parting with, so it should feel like you're getting a treat rather than feeling the same as when you're just buying a tin of beans.

You can see the same range of experiences in almost any market.

A lipstick can be picked up in the supermarket with the weekly shop or it can be a luxurious treat in a beautiful gold case, picked out for you by someone elegant who takes the time to find the right shade for you and then packs it in a lovely gift bag with some free samples of other items in the range.

You might say that a lipstick is a lipstick, but in times of austerity sales of luxury lipsticks go up. Women might not be able to afford the Dior outfit or the Chanel handbag, but they can afford the lipstick or the eye shadow.

Market research, part two

Now that you've looked at how people shop and more importantly, how companies sell to them, you need to bring your market research closer to home.

You need to see how they encourage the shopper to part with their money at Christmas. Obviously this can really only be done at Christmas and ideally you should start your research the year before you start your business, but that's not realistic! Luckily the shops start trying to sell us all the Christmas goodies months before the actual date so you still have time to gather some ideas and adapt them to your own needs as you start on your exciting first season.

The shopping mall itself plays a part in creating the Christmas atmosphere. The decorations sparkle, the Christmas tunes are playing and sometimes even the scents remind us of Christmas. Everything is designed to get you thinking about the holiday season and to prepare your mind for spending.

Then the shops play their part. Their windows have Christmas themed displays, sometimes very elaborate and expensive, the type of display that attracts people into the city centre or shopping mall every year just to enjoy the show. Every store, no matter how large or small is decorated for Christmas, showing their products and letting you imagine them as presents sitting under the tree.

Once you're inside the store the show continues - decorations, music, the Christmas theme, products packaged as ready to give Christmas gifts, free gift wrapping, special Christmas offers.

The fact is that every store – no matter how large or small – is after your Christmas budget. They want you to spend the money at their counters not their competitors.

Take a close look at how they do this and how they differ from one another.

Can you tell what their target audience is? How do they create an image?

Remember, they are the professionals at this and they have spent a great deal of time and money to create the look that they want, the look that will attract the target audience that they want and then get them to part with their money. Learn from their experience!

Although you might think that it is all a Christmas theme, once you begin to look closely, to really look rather than just be subconsciously affected by it, you'll be able to tell the difference in approach and how that relates to the different customers that they are targeting.

After all, the £ or $ store is targeting the Christmas spending the same as the largest department store, but they are definitely aiming for different customers.

What sort of colours have they used in their displays? The traditional holiday colours of red and green or white and silver can be used in very different ways to create different images.

If they have ready packaged gifts, how are they packaged – cheap and cheerful, aimed at children, glamorous, vintage, elegant, covered in snowmen and reindeer?

You've probably never thought about it before, but the designs aren't just accidental or the store manager's favourite style. Companies have huge budgets to spend on marketing and a lot of that money goes into designing their packaging and display. The way something looks has a very direct effect on who will buy it and how much they will pay for it. The value of a bottle of perfume is not in the actual liquid itself, it is in the image of the perfume, the way it is packaged the style of the bottle the way it is advertised and promoted. When you buy a bottle of couture perfume you are buying the image as much as the way it actually smells.

The same is true of the work that goes into marketing for Christmas.

Bath and body lotions are one of the staple Christmas gifts but there are many different ways of presenting them. You could simply go to the supermarket and buy a couple of bottles of shower gel off-the-shelf and wrap them in Christmas paper or you could go to one of the large department stores and buy a beautiful box that looks expensive and luxurious, which opens up to reveal two beautifully designed bottles of luxurious shower gel. You could choose a box whose design shows the latest cartoon character, or snowmen and reindeer, or a jokey bloke sprawled in his armchair by the Christmas tree, or a beautiful midnight blue with silver snowflakes finished with the rich satin ribbon.

All of these boxes are a gift of shower gel but the way they are presented means that you would buy them for very different people and you would pay very different prices for them.

So take a look at the way gifts are presented and in the way displays have been put together. The actual way they're displayed on a shelf or a counter or a table in the middle of the store, also makes a difference to the way the product is perceived.

If you walk into the store and are faced with a

freestanding table piled high with lots of identical gift boxes, you will subconsciously assume that this is a special offer and that they are being sold at a lower price than you would normally expect. No matter how elegantly it's done, there is the subconscious message being sent to you of pile them high sell them cheap. Of course the 'cheap' is a relative term and does depend on the type of store you are in. And expensive department store might mean that cheap, or good value is £50 instead of £100 while a cheap and cheerful outlet might mean £5 instead of £10.

So, are the items displayed on beautiful stands as individual pieces, or are they bundled together hanging from a wire spinner? Is the display crowded like an Aladdin's cave or does each individual gift have its own space?

What signals tell you the price range without even looking at the price?

Once you've actually looked at how things are sold and started to recognise what the subtle signals are in the selling process, you can begin to decide what signals you want to give to your potential customers and how you will go about that.

Who is your customer

Now that you have done some serious market research, you can begin to decide who your designs are is aimed at.

No matter how tempting it might seem, you cannot be all things to all people, you have to choose who your target audience is.

Where do you want to place yourself in what is - after all - a very crowded market?

You have to take a number of things into account.

Where will you be selling?

Who will your customer be?

Do you want to sell fashion designs or pieces of art that will last a lifetime?

You can either decide where you are going to sell and what type of customer you will have and what they will want, and set yourself up to design for that market.

Or you can decide what type of craft pieces you make or want to make and find an outlet that will attract the type of customer for your style and price range.

The problem is that it's not always easy - or possible - to find exactly the outlet you want - either in the area that you are based or at the rent that you can afford to pay - especially at first.

There's not much point deciding that you want to sell high end designer pieces at upwards of £100 a piece if you can't find a place to sell it from or Gothic chic in a quiet area that doesn't get a regular supply of Goths to adore your masterpieces.

The beauty about running a small business is that you can be adaptable. In fact that's one of your greatest strengths. You don't have to go through planning meetings, committees, getting approval and deciding on budgets, arranging purchasing, suppliers and mountains of other planning. You can get an idea, decide what you need to do and go and do it! See a trend and be selling it within weeks, sometimes within days if you have the parts. You can constantly adapt and change to a changing market.

So, probably the best way of deciding on your style is a mixture of what you like making and what price range you think will sell.

Don't be scared to be different. You don't simply want to churn out what everybody else is selling, or copy what you think is a popular style in the local supermarket. Put some of your own character into your work and that will help you create your own distinct style.

Whoever your customer is, one of the real delights of buying handmade pieces directly from the designer is the fact that you are buying something that you can't get in the local shops.

The Christmas season

Why is it necessary to consider Christmas Crafts as different to selling any craft?

Because the Christmas season is arguably the most important part of the year for your craft business.

That's true whether you consider yourself a Christmas specialist or whether you sell your handmade crafts all year round.

The Christmas season is important for all retailers and for some it is literally make or break.

Bad Christmas sales can mean that a big high street name disappears early in January or February.

So if it's that important for huge high street brands, it should be important for you too. You don't have to focus all your hopes on the Christmas season – you may be selling at craft fairs all through the year - but you should certainly aim to make as much as you can in this important part of the year.

It's that time of the year when you will find the most events, and some of the biggest events. The season runs from mid September to about the middle of December. The main out-of-town Christmas fairs are completed by the end of November or the very beginning of December and then events such as Christmas markets will run almost up to the holiday itself.

You need to think very seriously about the timing of events before you book them because you are not only investing your money, you are investing your time and you need to make the most of your time when you are selling in a specific season because it is limited and once Christmas Eve arrives your Christmas retail opportunity is over for another year.

You can always find some events in the traditional craft fair venues during the last couple of weeks before Christmas, but you have to think seriously before booking them. Will people come or will they be frantically looking for the last minute gifts and food at the shopping mall. The people that do come are probably more organised and are enjoying the atmosphere of a traditional Christmas fair, but are they going to buy anything or have they already done all their shopping.

There will always be some Christmas fairs that have become a traditional part of the Festive season. That people visit year after year, knowing that they can pick up the special pieces that they need to make the holiday complete. You just need to make sure that these are the event you invest your time in.

Preparation and planning

Some crafters spend most of the year preparing for the Christmas season, and for any crafter it can be the most hectic time of the year - in fact, it's best if you get your own Christmas family preparations done before September!

So if you plan on doing general craft fairs throughout the year, make sure that you have your Christmas gifts available in plenty of time for Christmas shoppers. December is too late for all but the last minute item, and shoppers that leave their gift shopping until the last few days are going to be panicking at a shopping mall not visiting your craft fair. The exception to this is when you have a stall at an event in the middle of town or a mall, such as a Christmas Market, then you do have the opportunity to catch the last minute shopper looking for something different – and that can be very profitable!

But as a general guide, most of your customers will begin to look seriously at planning their gift list by the time you have your craft fairs and events in September, which is why you should begin in September or October at the latest if you plan to concentrate on Christmas craft.

The end of the school summer holidays seems to trigger thoughts of Christmas shopping for a lot of people, so you need to have your potential gifts available for them at that time and you need to start planning, designing and making long before that.

The big high street stores start planning for the next Christmas just after the January sales!

And it's not only the fact that you might want to produce some Christmas designs – the actual type of purchasing changes as it gets towards the vital Christmas season.

During the rest of the year, your customer might be looking for a special birthday present, a new baby gift, a wedding, engagement or anniversary present or a treat for herself – but whichever it is, it's probably a single gift, which means that she can spend all her money on fewer items. Maybe some gifts to take home from a holiday, maybe there are a couple of birthdays in the month. But in my experience, it is easier to sell more expensive, individual pieces during the main part of the year.

Once it comes to September, customers are thinking of Christmas gifts. Gifts plural, so each one has to be more considered. Some will still be large gifts – large in value, not necessarily size – but many will be smaller, lower priced presents. Gifts for school teachers, neighbours, people at work, Secret Santas, small gifts for friends and family. Many of these will have a set price point and your customer will be looking for something that is different but that still falls into this previously decided price bracket.

You should take this into account when you're designing your Christmas stock. They don't have to be obviously Christmas designs, in fact you should only make a proportion of your pieces with overtly seasonal designs – not everyone wants to buy everything covered in snowmen and reindeer!

The Christmas season is crowded with products as anyone who has looked around a shopping mall will know. However it is crowded with thousands of very similar products and the great opportunity for any craft worker is to create designs that are different.

When you are planning your designs you should bear this in mind

Where will you sell?

This book is mainly aimed at the process of selling for and during the Christmas season. This means that you will be looking at selling opportunities from about September right through to Christmas Eve.

This is one of the busiest times for craft events and of course there are plenty of craft fairs to choose from, some small and held in schools or church halls and some very large lasting three or four days and held in exhibition centres.

But if you plan to specialise your business on Christmas selling you need to make the very most of this short, intense season. So you should also consider the Christmas markets which many some towns now hold. They can last anything from one week to many weeks, some of them start in mid-November and go through to Christmas Eve and are a serious commitment of time and investment and probably not the place to start your business.

However you can take a stall at a weekly market

or if you are in the right area at a number of different markets spending a different day in each town for a number of weeks leading up to Christmas.

You can also find a number of farmers markets many of which do allow you to take a craft stall and again these will normally occur once a week or sometimes once a month.

Shopping malls often hold special events where they open their doors to craft makers for a few days. This encourages more shoppers to visit and gives you the opportunity to place your designs in front of thousands of shoppers.

The Christmas season is the focus for many events, many charities will organise Christmas events that include craft stalls, local schools also organise events which are either focused on craft fairs or would include craft stalls.

You should also think out of the box. You can often arrange to give talks or demonstrations about your craft and of course take some of your designs with you so that people can make purchases if they want. Many societies and groups have a series of speakers in during the year, contact them to see if they are interested in you giving a talk for their Christmas meetings.

Retirement homes are often looking for people who can visit them and giving interesting talks as well as some retail opportunities to their residents, again, contact them and ask if they are interested in some Christmas entertainment.

Of course there are other ways of selling your

handmade designs nowadays. People often think of selling online first when they are planning a new business, through etsy, eBay, Amazon or your own website.

You could decide to sell through craft and gift shops or wholesale to other outlets. And that's fine, but there's still plenty of chances to sell directly to your customers face-to-face and if you intend to do most of your selling in the 3 to 4 month Christmas season, then selling face-to-face rather than online gives you the control over your selling season. It's very difficult to turn your website on and off.

When should you start planning your Christmas bookings?

Ideally in January!

Although you can often make bookings at quite short notice, especially for smaller events that might be planned close to the date, or if there have been cancellations at some of the more established events, many bookings are made about a year in advance, especially for the popular, successful events.

So you should be prepared to start planning your Christmas campaign in January to make sure that you are at the most successful events.

Craft fairs.

This is probably the section you will think of first when you decide to sell your handmade designs direct to the customer face-to-face.

You've probably visited quite a number of craft

fairs over the years, but once you step onto the other side of the counter there is actually quite a lot to know about craft fairs.

There's a huge variety in the type of event, the size of event, how much rent you will have to pay, how many days you will have to commit and what is expected from you as a craftsperson.

At one end of the scale, you will find small local events, where you can simply book a six-foot table and pay about £20-£30 for the day. Tables are normally supplied, although for some fairs you do have to supply your own, in which case a wallpaper pasting table is normally first choice but you'll probably move on to a more sturdy version after you've completed a few fairs.

As a general guide, most of these fairs start at about 10am and close at about 4pm with the venue being open from about 8am to 5pm to allow you time to set up and then clear away again afterwards.

The organisers for most of these smaller events will expect you to be on time, stay to the end of the fair, pay your table rent and sell only your own hand made goods. Many of them will also require you to have public and product liability insurance which you certainly should have for your own protection.

Many of these organisers run fairs throughout the year, either a regular event at a specific venue or a programme of events at different venues that repeats throughout the year. As you book more fairs you will get to know more crafts people and they tend to be very generous with their knowledge and will let you know who else to contact about different events.

Customers are often very loyal to a series of events and they will follow them to different venues or to the same venue year after year, so you automatically have a very good opportunity of building up a regular following. If you develop a distinctive style, people will collect your designs and comeback season after season looking for your latest designs, which of course is a very good reason to keep your designs fresh.

Other organisers will arrange larger events at a specific venue, often their own, once or twice a year. These can be at garden centres, hotels and shopping centres, or even in town centres. They will normally be two or three day events and will quite often cost from £150 a day and upwards. You will definitely require public and product liability insurance before you're allowed to book and any electrical equipment you use will have to have a PAT certificate (portable appliance testing).

Some of these events will be craft and gift fairs which can have pros and cons. It means that you can sell items you have bought in, but it also means that your beautiful handmade pieces will be competing directly against mass-market designs from China.

A larger event will attract more people, which means more potential customers. As well as being prepared to speculate more time and money you will also have to have more stock, so that you can make the most of the larger number of people passing your stall.

School or church fairs

School and church fairs are quite often much shorter events, possibly only two or three hours during the afternoon or in the evening. They can also be midweek, whereas most craft fairs are focused on the weekend. This means that they are easy to fit in around your main schedule. You can quite often leave a large event at about 4pm on Saturday, go and do a small school fair in the evening, and be back at the large event on Sunday morning. Try not to do this too often as it can be very tiring!

Although they are smaller events, and they will cost you less rent, they are often quite well attended by people who have every intention of purchasing. Small fairs tend to happen at certain times of the year, around Easter, in the summer and for Christmas. Once you are on an organisers list, you will tend to become a regular. doing the same fairs year after year, hopefully attracting a loyal following. Many charity events also fall into the same pattern.

Christmas markets

Christmas markets are quite obviously held at Christmas!

They've become very popular in recent years, and they tend to be organised by towns and cities to be held as part of the general Christmas festivities.

Although they do vary from town to town, many of them last a number of weeks and take the form of stalls in the town centre. Sometimes they are the standard market stalls under canvas while some towns set individual wooden huts and others set aside a section of the indoor market or an indoor shopping centre.

If the markets are outside or in a marquee, you have to be prepared for the weather. Being outside in the winter can certainly be cold! You will also have to set up and dismantle your stall each day as obviously you cannot leave anything open overnight in the middle of the town centre.

In a Christmas market you are competing directly with all the other shops and big stores in town rather than competing with other crafters. Your designs and way you present them have to be able to stand on their own against all the other products competing for the money in the shopper's wallet.

The plus points in this that it is easy to see how your designs differ from the mass produced products that are available in stores. When buying a gift or a decoration from you the customer will be getting something unique, something handcrafted, something that cannot simply be bought in one of the stores.

The other benefit of doing a Christmas market, is that you are going to the shoppers rather than hoping that the shoppers will come to your craft fair.

At this time of the year most people are in full panic mode trying to get far too many things done in far too short a time, which means that huge numbers of them will simply go to the stores or the shopping mall to blitz their Christmas shopping in one go. If you concentrate on craft fairs you have no chance of getting these customers, but if you are easily available where they are already shopping they have the choice of choosing something different from you rather than the same old same old from the stores.

Christmas markets can be a huge investment in both money and time. Some of the markets will start in the middle of November and run through to Christmas Eve. If you do choose to take on this kind of commitment you will be depending on one particular event and one particular venue because you simply will not have time-or the energy-to do many other events.

Some of the organisers will allow you to take blocks of time at their market or certain days each week but you will have to check with the organiser as they do vary.

House parties

Selling by party plan at house parties can be a very successful way of selling your handcrafted designs.

Some of the more traditional party plan has gone out of fashion, after all there is only so many storage containers that you really want! But that doesn't mean that the idea of party plan is out of date, far from it, it just means that people are looking for more unusual reasons to have a party.

Unique handmade designs are ideal for this. Hand crafted items are a very easy present to give to others and you can have enough of a price range to make it comfortable for everybody at the party. Because although some people can quite comfortably afford to spend £70 or £80, in these more economically challenging times there are many others who would be relieved to be able to just spend £5 or £10 without embarrassment.

Once you have started doing house parties, they do have a tendency to feed of themselves, in fact that's the whole idea of a successful party plan business. Someone, preferably two people at the party will book parties of their own and invite different selections of people, which will lead on again to more bookings and more new customers.

Obviously the best way to start is if you can persuade some of your friends to hold a party for you. But you can also arrange to work with someone who already does party plan with a different product and is willing to let you join them.

You should also advertise the fact that you do parties at every other event that you attend.

There are a few main things you need to do, to create a successful party plan business.

Make it easy for the host to have a party.

Create invitations or leaflets that they can hand out to their friends. People need to know what to expect to see for sale at the party and how much they expect the items to cost, so that they have an idea of the price ranges. They also need to know when and where it is. It's a good idea to put some photos of your designs onto the invitation and if you have a website put the address on so that they can go and have a look at the type of handmade designs you have for sale. And do emphasise that it is handmade, by you rather than just mass produced and available at the market.

Make it worthwhile for the host to have a party.

She will be going to quite a lot of trouble and some expense, providing wine and nibbles at least for her guests, as well as putting the time in to arrange the party. So it has to be worth her while. You can decide on the exact style of your incentive, but generally it will be something like a percentage of the value of your total sales in the evening to be spent on her own personal order. The percentage is up to you, but is normally somewhere between 10% and 20%. You could also decide to give a bonus for each person that books a further party, or a special offer only available to the organiser on the evening. The more creative you can be, the more successful you should be in booking future parties. After all, people are more likely to book a party of their own if they feel it's going to be worthwhile to them.

Make it easy to set up your party.

For both your sake and your host's sake, you don't want to spend two hours setting up your display! Design an easy and time efficient way of carrying and setting out your range. You have a limited amount of time and space when doing a house party, so don't try to take every design you've ever made. Decide from your experience, what your bestsellers are and make sure that you have them together with enough variety for people to have a choice, but not so much that it overwhelms them.

Make it interesting for the host and her guests.

Don't just put your designs out and expect them to sell themselves. Don't just stand in a corner like a wallflower. Give a short talk that explains something about your designs, what makes it special, what makes it different, can you personalise your pieces. Give them an idea of the price range, show how you can put a collection together. Talk about how you can design special pieces for them.

Make it easy for the guests to make a purchase.

Most party plan businesses rely on people placing an order and receiving it at a later date. Personally I always have my selection of my handmade designs for them to take away on the night. Although there are some times when a number of people want the same design, this is quite unusual, after all the beauty of handcrafted work is that it is different for everyone. If it does happen, then I will take the order and post the piece out to them directly rather than expecting the host of the party to do the deliveries for me.

If you are doing parties close to Christmas it is even more important for your customers to know that they will have the gifts in time to hand them over – and don't assume that will be Christmas day. Many gifts need to be exchanged before that, at Christmas parties, on the last day or school or when visiting friends. Some will have to be posted to relatives , so make sure that you understand when they are needed for and that the customer understands when you plan to deliver special order pieces.

Finally make it easy and worthwhile for the guests to book a party of their own. The life blood of a party plan business is to continually book new parties. If you book one party from each party that you do, your business will stay level. If you book two parties from each party you do your business will grow. But if you don't book any parties, your business will die.

Markets

As we discussed earlier, there are quite a range of Christmas markets nowadays, but this type of event doesn't suit every craft worker. They often involve a large investment in both time and money and that can be very restrictive as well as the fact that you can limit yourself to the success or failure of a single, long event.

But that doesn't mean that markets are off your list altogether.

Many towns hold regular markets throughout the year rather than just during the Christmas season, and you can often book your space for the September to December period rather than having to commit to the whole year. Some of them run almost every day, although you can choose to book one or two days a week rather than being committed to one market seven days a week. Others, such as farmers markets, will only be on once a month and there are a whole range of other markets that will run one day every week.

Some of these are general markets, some of them are farmers markets, and some of them are craft markets. Which type you might decide to take a stall at is entirely up to you. Different markets suit different crafters, but there are some general rules that apply to any of them.

Most market organisers will supply the stalls, which are normally a metal framework covered by a (mostly) waterproof canvass. They will also normally supply the table top for you to set your product out on. You will have to supply your own covers, and of course you won't have electricity in most cases.

Markets take place on every day of the week. Some towns have a weekly market, whereas others are held on every day of the week. Many market traders have a weekly route around their local towns, setting up shop every morning in the next town. As a crafter it is highly unlikely that you will follow that pattern as you need time to create your product, so you would probably only do two or maybe three regular days a week or concentrate all your bookings into the holiday season.

Some of the indoor markets have space allocated for a specialist Craft fair that they hold once a month. Although these are held in markets, they do follow more the pattern of the craft fair. You will have a 6 foot table as your stall and you probably will have an electrical supply.

Markets whether indoor or outside, are very open areas, with the public milling around, rather than people who have chosen to come into a craft fair. This means that you can have a much wider range of potential customers, but it also means that you have to be more aware of the risk of shoplifters. Make sure that any expensive pieces are out of the way of sticky fingers and take care of your cash.

If you are planning on doing many markets, it is worth joining the National Market Traders Federation, membership of which gives you public and product liability insurance, as well as many other benefits.

Talks to social and church groups

There are many groups who are constantly looking for people to give talks at their monthly meetings.

Obviously, many of the people who will give talks will require some payment to cover their costs.

If you are able to take a selection of your products with you that are available for their members to purchase, then you can offer to give the talk without charge. You are taking the risk that you will give the talk and not take any money, but personally, I have never had this happen. In fact, many of these events can be extremely lucrative.

I always give a gift to the organisation that they can use as a raffle prize, sometimes on the night, sometimes with a raffle to be held at a later date, it's their choice. As a craft worker, you can give a gift that is worth a lot more than it costs you to produce.

Many members of such groups are members of more than one, so as always, do make sure that everyone has your contact details. As with party plan, you will find that you make bookings from bookings.

Again, as with party plan, make it easy to set up your display.

For both your sake and the group's sake, you don't want to spend two hours setting up your stand! They will often only have access to the hall about half an hour before the start of their meeting. Normally, they will deal with group business, such as reading the minutes first and then hand the rest of the meeting over to you. You will have to be able to set up your display quickly and quietly. You will also need to be able to pack it away quickly once the meeting is over.

Design an easy and time efficient way of carrying and setting out your range, don't try to take every design you've ever made. You will also have to be flexible about how you set out your display as you won't know beforehand what type of tables they will supply.

Decide from your experience what your bestsellers are and make sure that you have them, together with enough variety for people to have a choice, but not so much that it overwhelms them. You'll find over time that your bestsellers vary from venue to venue and event type to event type. Keep a record of what you sell so that you can see any patterns that emerge.

Make it interesting for the group, you are there to give a talk after all. Don't just put your designs out and expect it to sell itself, selling anything is supposed to be a bonus at this type of event. Give a short talk that explains something about your designs, what makes it special, what makes it different?

For this type of talk, you can get more personal, because they are not just interested in buying the designs, they are interested in what drew you into handcrafted work. How did you learn? How long have you been making designs? Where do you get your design inspiration? What made you decide to set up business?

Give them an idea of the price range, show how you can put a set together. Talk about how you can design special pieces for them.

Once you have finished your talk, which you should keep to about 20 to 30 minutes, be prepared for a rush! This is not a leisurely day long craft fair, everybody wants to be served within about 15 minutes before they rush off to get a bus, meet someone who's giving them a lift, or just get home!

These talks can take place during the day or in the evenings and at any time of the week, depending on what type of group you are talking to. So you can fit quite a number into your calendar. They are often booked over a year in advance as the social secretary arranges the diary for the year.

Selling online

Although this book mainly concentrates on selling your Christmas crafts face-to-face to your customer at craft fairs, markets and other events, many people also combine this with an on-line presence.

When you are selling on-line you will probably be actively selling all year round rather than just for the festive season. A website, or even a presence on one of the main selling platforms has to be nurtured and built over time, so it's really not something that you can turn on in September and expect to achieve great sales.

Selling online does not suit every product or every craft worker but if you do sell on-line, either on your own website or on something like Etsy, eBay or Amazon, or any of the other specialist websites, there are some things that you need to take into account for selling during the festive season.

Doing your Christmas shopping online is

becoming more and more popular as people have less and less time in their lives. Year on year the value of purchases online has increased by a huge amount and if you are able to, it is well worth taking advantage of this growing trend.

Many of the business decisions for selling at Christmas are the same whether you sell face-to-face or online.

You have to decide on your designs, on your packaging, on your special offers.

You have to decide whether you will produce specific Christmas designs or whether you will repackage your existing designs into Christmas gifts.

But there is one area in particular that you don't have to consider when selling face-to-face, but which is absolutely central to your business plan for selling online.

Delivery.

Once a customer has chosen the gift they want and have gone through your system to order and pay for it, you have to physically get it to them.

Obviously this is something you have to consider with online selling at any time of the year but there are some extra things you have to think about when you're selling during the festive season.

There are always stories in the papers about the terrible on-line seller and how they ruined Christmas by not getting the presents out on time!

Timing is one of the most important things.

You would be amazed – or probably horrified -

at how little some people think about actual delivery times.

I run my business and dispatch parcels from England. At most times of the year it will take a package about two weeks to reach a customer in the USA or Australia - which I make very clear on my website.

Obviously it can take a lot longer during the Christmas Season. The last recommended posting days for Australia is normally the first week in December, and for the United States, the second week in December.

But unfortunately almost every year will bring in some Christmas orders on the 21st and 22nd of December to be delivered to either of these two countries. Of course they won't get there in time, which I have to explain to the customer and offer to cancel the order.

And the same thing will happen more locally, within the UK – orders placed on Christmas Eve. I cannot get the package them in time for Christmas unless they live down the road from me. There isn't a delivery on Christmas Day, no matter how much someone is willing to pay!

Although you can't allow for every individual person, you must do your very best to make it as clear as possible what the last posting dates are for each country.

Your local mail service should be able to give you these details and you should display them as clearly as possible on your website or in your descriptions.

If you don't offer special delivery options on your items during the year, you should add them for the holiday season, again allowing for those who like to do their shopping last minute.

You might also want to make some contingency plans in case your normal delivery service suffers any problems during this important time. After all more than any other time of the year, it is vital that deliveries arrive on time. Christmas presents that arrive just before New Year and not only useless they will get you a very bad reputation. Postal strikes have been the cause of many business failures over the years.

Although you may have to charge more for alternative delivery services, you should list them so that customers can make a choice.

Many businesses also extend their return period for the holiday season, choosing some point in the lead up to Christmas to extend their return period from the normal 14 or 30 days and instead allowing customers to return items after Christmas Day, normally sometime early in the New Year.

Of course all of these decisions are entirely up to you and have to be made to suit your business and your own personal requirements, but you should at least consider them.

Presenting Yourself

Setting out your stall

When you're selling face-to-face, whether it's at markets, Christmas fair, school or church events, craft fairs, or house parties - your main display counter will be a table.

When you actually book a craft fair, do check exactly what you will be supplied with. Is it simply the space?

Will you have to take your own table and chairs or are they supplied? Do check, don't just assume.

You want to know exactly what you will be supplied with when you make your reservation. Some organisers -not many - supply simply the space, you will have to take your own table and chairs.

Others supply a table only if you book one specifically. So do check the details. The last thing you want to do is arrive early one morning and find you have nothing to set your stall out on or nowhere to sit for the entire day.

Most craft fair organisers do actually supply a

table and two chairs, but it's then up to you to turn a very basic, often tatty table into an attractive stand.

The standard table is 6ft long x 2ft wide and is often a trestle table. You normally have space behind the table for you to stand in and to put your chairs. You also normally have some space to the side, or both sides, between you and the next stand – but you don't always have this space, so don't rely on it. You can turn up first thing in the morning and find that all the stalls are in a single, solid line!

The space between the tables is to allow you and your neighbour to enter and leave your stand easily, to allow you to step from behind your stand and talk to a customer or replenish your display. Don't fill it with an extra stand or rail, or push your chair in front to use as more display space. Space invaders cause bad feeling and you'll find that other crafters no longer want to be quite so helpful. Crafters are normally very helpful to each other and you'll need the support – especially if you are on your own. Neighbours normally cover each other's stands so that you can get a coffee or take a quick break.

Some organisers will provide you with extra space free of charge if you will demonstrate your craft and this can be well worth doing - showing how to make something always seems to draw a crowd. But you will definitely need to have someone else with you to make sales while you are busy demonstrating

The table is your shop window and you only have a few seconds to catch the attention of the passing crowd. So you must make a good first impression. Make your public take that all important second look.

You may find yourself using tables from hotel dining rooms, factory canteens or, as I said earlier, they are very often trestle tables.

As a guide, a standard table will be about 6ft long by 2ft wide, and remember -you have to carry and put up the rest of your stand yourself, so you need something that looks good without taking a small lorry to transport it and an hour to put together.

As I said, all tables are slightly different because on the whole, organisers use whatever they have to hand.

So although you will normally find yourself using the standard 6x2ft table, you might have a different length or width or even a round table (occasionally) or even some school desks placed together, because they do tend to use what is available. So be prepared to adapt your display on the day.

I find that it is easier to make up the display with a variety smaller stands that can be adapted to make the best use of the space and shape available, rather than be restricted with a design that will only fit a certain size and shape of stall. Smaller display stands are also easier to pack and carry!

Many fairs also supply electricity, although with

some you have to book it specifically. This means that you can light your product, which is well worth doing as it will attract attention. You will need to carry extension cables as well as your lights, because some but not all organisers supply the electricity to your stall while with others you will have to have cables to reach the wall sockets.

This basic table is your shop window and it's up to you to design an eyecatching but workable setup to turn something that can be quite tatty into a wonderful and affective shop front.

And in exactly the same way as a shop window display in the High Street or shopping mall, your display has to attract the attention of your potential customer as they walk around the fair.

It has to help you compete against the stalls on either side of you and opposite you, as well as anyone else selling a similar product.

With any type of selling, whether it's a full page advert in a magazine costing thousands of pounds, or your craft stall - you only have a few seconds to catch the attention of the passing crowd, so you have to make a good first impression that will make your public take that all important second look that will lead to them actually approaching your stand and looking at your designs.

Even if you book a space at a large professional exhibition, you will still normally start with a table inside your booth. You can move on to a display of shelves and glass cabinets if you are going to be concentrating your business on exhibition space, but you won't begin your career with that type of investment and many craftworkers never have the need for large professional display equipment.

So - a 6 foot table. How do you turn that into an attractive shopfront?

You need some basic things:

A cover

Height

Lighting

The cover.

The cover is quite straightforward. It wants to be big enough to cover your table to the floor. It looks very amateurish to have it hanging in midair. You want to create your own space, and while the top of the table is your selling space, under the table is your store room and you don't want to leave the store room wide open for the public to see!

You can use standard tablecloths or sheets if you need to but it's worth setting yourself up properly in the first place.

Find a fabric shop, preferably one that sells upholstery and curtain fabric and buy some sheeting.

Sheeting is wide enough to cover the top and front of your stand and you can buy enough length to stretch past each end of the table so that you can create a tidy corner with the aid of some hospital corners and safety pins. (For those who don't know, a hospital corner is a way of tidily folding the bedsheets!)

You will also have a choice of colours. The

colour of your cloth will be the basis of your whole look and is a major part of your overall style.

Crisp white – (which needs to be kept spotlessly clean)

Elegant black

Rich burgundy.

Cool blue

Funky yellow

Pretty pink

Of course if you are concentrating on crafts for the Christmas season, the image that your shopfront gives is a vital part of your business.

It has to look festive.

You can go for the very traditional green and red colour scheme or you might want to go for a white and silver snow effect. Almost any colour can be adapted to create a festive feel and some are more obvious and easier to work with than others.

Think about how the department store windows were dressed for Christmas and use that knowledge when you are creating your own display.

Whatever colour you choose you will want the rest of your display to work with it, so it is a very important decision. Don't be tempted to grab the first thing you find and think that will do. If you don't put some thought into it at this stage you will end up replacing your covers quite quickly which is an unnecessary expense.

It's also worth buying some extra fabric so that you can use this to cover any extra boxes that you will use.

If you can't find exactly the colour you've decided on, buy white sheeting and dye it to the colour you want. If you do choose this method make sure that you prepare more fabric than you think you'll need. There will be times when you book more space at a fair and you'll need cloths for at least a 12ft display.

Height

Once you have the groundwork set, you have to decide on how to display your goods.

Clearly this depends to a very large extent on the product itself. Are you selling small, delicate items or large, flat or three dimensional crafts?

A flat 6 x 2 table with designs just lying on it will look - well flat!

Boring and uninteresting. Dull.

You get the idea? It will look amateurish and apart from anything else, you're limiting your display space

Think back to that shopping centre. Did any of the stores have their designs lying flat on the bottom of the window display? No! They have hundreds of pounds worth of display stands layered up on beautiful shelving to show everything off.

Your version doesn't need cost hundreds of pounds, there are lots of ways that you can create the same sort of effect. Be creative.

Height adds interest, it adds variation, it adds space.

A good basic rule to work by is that people tend to notice things that are at eye level. Brands spend a fortune to obtain the eye level shelving position in supermarkets.

So you want to draw their attention to your display by forming some kind of higher background leading inwards towards the main display.

One of the easiest ways to add height is to unpack the boxes you carry everything in, turn them upside down and cover them in smaller cloths that match your main table cover.

If you do use this method, then your choice of storage box becomes a bit more important. You want to select suitable sizes, not too big and not too small, and possibly a variety of sizes. You also want to choose boxes with flat bases, so that they will create good, stable shelving.

One of the best types of box is a sturdy cardboard case that fruit and vegetables are used to deliver them to the greengrocers and supermarkets. They are strong, often have good handle slots for carrying, they stack on top of one another, they have flat bases and they're free!

Once you drape your cloth over them, no one will guess how humble your beautiful shelving really is.

You can build a framework to stand at the back of the table. This works basically like a large open book standing at right angles and can be made of two notice boards hinged together, or it can be a more open structure such as trellis held in a frame.

You can design this part of your stand so that your lighting will clip to your frame or to allow for free standing spot lights. Lighting that is directed down onto the display is a very effective style of illuminations and avoids the problem of blinding your customer. Many products can be transformed from something rather ordinary into a glittering Aladdin's Cave with some simple light and again, it will make your stand look professional.

You can also have individual stands for smaller items such as jewellery or ceramic ornaments, or a rail effect if you are selling clothing. Just remember that you must have permission if you want to use a stand additional to your table space and you will normally have to pay for the extra space. Do remember to take you neighbours into account, you should never encroach on their space or block customers from their stand.

You can also buy a selection of clear acrylic stands in various shapes and sizes and these can be very effective for smaller products.

Look around and think out of the box. There are lots of cup cake stands around at the moment and they can make very effective display stands for small items.

As we are concentrating on the Festive season, you could use Christmas trees to display your products, or tree branches painted in white or silver that you have hang your work from.

Whatever you choose, you should try to avoid the single level, table top display - people don't always look down - they look around as they walk though the hall or marquee and you need to catch their attention as they wander.

But also remember that you have to be able to carry and assemble the display. Always keep that in mind as you create elaborate creations in your imagination!

Lighting

It's very tempting to ignore lighting, especially when you are first starting out, but that is a mistake.

Think of the way jewellery glitters in jewellery shop windows. It's not just that they're diamonds, gemstones and precious metals, they are very well lit!

And when you look at other stands around you at your first craft show, you will notice that those crafters who know what they are doing - have lights!

When you are deciding on your lights, there are certain things to take into account. They need to be sturdy and easy to carry around. Take the weight into account as well, you will have to carry them from fair to fair and at times, you will have to carry them upstairs or the length of long marquees.

Look around at various shops for your lights. You don't need to go for special - and normally expensive - professional shop display lighting. Nowadays, you can find plenty of choice in home decor or office supply stores.

The style of lighting will depend on your overall

display. If you have a large sturdy framework, you can clip lights to that. If your display is more open, you probably need freestanding lights.

The right lighting will really make your stand and your beautiful, handmade crafts stand out. And remember, the initial stage of making a sale is getting a customer's attention in the first place.

You will also need to have extension cables in your equipment pack, as you will often have to connect to the power supply at a distance.

Many organisers will require that you have your electrical equipment tested. A PAT certificate (portable appliance testing) is required for each piece of equipment and lasts 12 months.

If you are planning to sell at markets where electricity if not available, look around and see if you can find some suitable battery powered lighting. New technology has made some of this lighting very effective.

There are all sorts of other things, you can add to your stand to attract attention and what you choose will depend on your style. You could decide to display one of your main pieces on a Lazy Susan so that it catches the light as it turns, or you could use a digital photo frame to showcase some of your other designs.

Exhibition Banners

However you design your table, the first task of your stand is to be noticed.

You may well be in hall with 50, 70 or over 100 other craft stalls, so you want people to notice yours. You want them to stop, look at your designs and of course you want them to buy. But if you don't attract them in the first place none of that can happen.

The exhibition banner displayed behind your table is a great way of doing this. It's an advert that people can see from a distance. You can include pictures of your designs on the banner so that they have an idea of what you have on offer before they risk becoming too close!

Many of the copy and print centres and some of the big stationery stores now produce this kind of banner or stand for you from about £50. So if you're planning on doing a number of events this can be a very good investment. Do think of the design carefully. If you use a banner this will be your largest visual advert, so you want to make sure that it is sending the message you want and that it is giving people the correct idea about your style.

To show or not to show?

Now that you have your stand structure organised you have to decide how to place your product on it.

There is a great temptation to put absolutely everything on display at the same time, but you should avoid this.

Use the curtained space you have created beneath the table as your stock room and the table top for the presentation of your product.

The way you present your display has a direct

effect on the way it is seen by the customer. Not just in a straight forward visual way but subconsciously as well.

In general, a crowded display tends to imply that the product is cheap. Think of the `pile them high, sell them cheap' methods of some supermarkets. They don't just choose that style by accident, a lot of money has gone into researching the effect it has on the image of the product or the retailer.

At the other end of the scale, think of the way high quality, expensive products are displayed in the department stores. A single piece of crystal will stand on its own, the window display will present two or three outfits in a set piece. The space left around the product is as important as the product itself if you want to create an image of quality.

So the general rule is:-

A cluttered effect - bargain basement prices and low quality products

A very elegant display - high quality and high prices

You probably want to pitch your product somewhere between the two. After all, you want to get the right price but you don't want to scare people off!

Another very good reason for keeping some of the stock back in reserve is to encourage a customer to *buy now*.

If the potential customer sees only one example of the glass, jumper, picture or teddy bear that they particularly like, they are more likely to purchase it straight away rather than leave it until later, because it might be gone when they get back.

This is doubly important. It means that you get the sale straight away, and it avoids the problem of the well meaning customer never returning to make the purchase.

.

Your Christmas Shopfront

Many of the guidelines for setting out your stall can be used at any time of the year. After all when ever you are at an event you want to attract customers and make sales.

But Christmas is different and you should make the most of it. People's method of shopping at Christmas is different, they have bigger lists they are not just browsing they are shopping for a purpose and you have lots of competition for their money so you need to make the most of the attention you manage to get from them.

Setting out your Christmas shopfront is your way of attracting their attention.

Again, take a leaf out of the expert's book. The department stores spend thousands of pounds decorating their windows. The shopping centres make a big feature of their Christmas decorations, and town centres make an entire event out of turning on the Christmas lights. They do this because it attracts customers, and it puts them in the Christmas mood, which makes them think of buying presents and spending money.

So join in.

Decorate your table. Use tinsel or fairy lights along the front. Maybe you have enough room for a miniature Christmas tree or some snowflakes and if the style is right for your image you could even wear a Santa hat.

Whatever you decide, make your stall festive, encourage people to think of buying Christmas gifts when they see your display.

Although serious Christmas shopping starts in September, it's normally better to wait until the beginning of November before you pull out all the stops in your Christmas display, but it is effective.

When potential customers see your stall looking like a Christmas display they will subconsciously think Christmas.

Some organisers are very good about creating the right atmosphere and so are some crafters, but a surprising number are not and if that is the case, your display will really stand out at the fair and will at least create the right atmosphere around you and your products.

Carry the theme through your whole display. If you have decided to use beautiful gift boxes as part of your promotion, display them on your table, make them look like a wonderful display of presents. Don't hide them away with the idea that customers should know you'll package the gift for them.

Think how the stores display all the beautiful gift wrapped boxes that they have on offer at this time of the year. Very often the products inside them are nothing special. Body lotions, shower gels, hand creams, maybe a china mug with some sweets inside it, maybe a tie and some cufflinks. Many of these wonderful looking gift boxes contain quite ordinary products, but they are packaged in a beautiful way in beautiful boxes with ribbon around them. It's easy to just buy them, take them home and put them under the tree.

People are always short of time, especially at Christmas time, and buying this type of ready to give gifts is so much easier to do. It takes the thinking and the work out of the process, so customers are attracted to anything that will save them time and make life easy.

Yes, it would be cheaper to buy a nice box and all the body lotions and package them yourself, but people don't do that, they pay extra to have it done for them.

So when they see your designs beautifully packaged and presented, it will automatically look more like a gift and that's the effect you want.

When you're selling at the Christmas season it's all about getting the sales.

People want to buy gifts.

They will part with their money.

They have to go home with all the presents they need - the stocking fillers, small gifts for friends and neighbours, the gifts for teachers and for work colleagues as well as great aunt Sally and mother's next door neighbour.

They have to find these gifts on the list and they

will spend their money somewhere. Your main aim at this time of the year is to get them to spend it with you.

That is why you invest money in taking a stand at the fair in the first place, so invest a little more in creating beautiful packaging.

Selling the message

I know I'm labouring the point here, but it's because it's such an important point!

If you have decided to focus your business on selling for Christmas you need to make the very most of every selling opportunity you have during this vital holiday season. If you sell Christmas crafts, once Christmas Eve comes, your selling opportunities are over until the next September so you need to ring every drop out that important retail season.

Focus on every detail of your promotional plan and make sure that everyone who passes your stall can understand what you have on offer.

If you have decided to use beautiful gift boxes as part of your promotion, display them on your table.

Make life easier for your potential customer. Everyone always has too much to do in the lead up to Christmas, so if you can solve some of the customers problems by making the gift giving easier, or the decoration of the house easier, or decorating the Christmas table easier they will willingly spend their money with you, because at the bottom line you are selling them time.

Buying a beautifully decorated christmas cake from you means that the customer doesn't have to go home and worry about creating the cake herself.

Finding a gorgeous selection of personalised Christmas stockings on your stand, means that she doesn't have to start searching the stores for something ordinary that then requires decoration.

And when they see your designs, beautifully packaged and presented it will automatically look like a gift, better still a gift that doesn't require packaging. And that's the effect you want.

This might also be the time to decide to use one of the price promotions. Again, very often used by stores. The most popular one is 3 for 2 - of course remember that it's always the lowest priced item that is free!

This is another time you should learn from the experts. They have found that, particularly at Christmas, this promotion will encourage people to buy two items, rather than just one. In fact, you can find yourself spending longer in front of the shelves wondering who you will give the extra two gifts to and what you should choose, when it would be much quicker and cheaper to just pick the one you wanted in the first place. But that's the point. It works. So if the big stores can make the most of it - so can you.

Of course, do remember that they are all priced to cover the cost of the three items, even though as a shopper you feel that you are getting a bargain, and there's that wonderful magic word again –

FREE!

So if you decide to use this promotion, do make sure that you work out your prices correctly. You're not actually in the business of giving away designs – even at Christmas!

When you're selling at the Christmas season it's all about getting the sales.

People want to buy gifts.

They will part with their money.

They have to go home with all the presents they need.

The stocking fillers.

Small gifts for friends and neighbours.

The gifts for teachers.

The gifts for loved ones.

People also want to decorate their homes and offices for Christmas, so they are out there looking for tree decorations, table decorations, crackers, Christmas wreaths and garlands.

They want the special Christmas foods, the beautiful decorated cakes, the chutneys, the truffles and luxury chocolates, the cookies, the sweet mince pies and gingerbread houses.

They will spend their money somewhere, and your main aim at this time of the year is to get them to spend it with you. That is why you invest money in taking a stand at the fair in the first place.

The rest of your equipment bag

There are other things that you need to make sure you have with you when you set out to do a show.

A cash float. Yes, I know the plan is to take money, but you also need to have some with you in the first place. Most people get their money from cash machines nowadays, so they will be presenting you with beautifully crisp £10 and £20 notes, you will need to have some change for them if you want to make a sale. Make sure you have a good selection of £5 notes, £1 coins, silver and copper if you're going to set your prices at £4.99, £9.99, £14.99 etc.

You also want to keep your cash safe. So you will need a cash box to make it easy to sort out your coins, and a bag that you can keep attached to you to keep all the hundreds of £10 notes safe.

You'll need a calculator to add up all the sales, a note book to keep a record of them and also to take notes for special orders that you will be sending out, so of course you'll need a pen!

Depending on how you have decided to display your designs, you might need a supply of price labels, some paper bags or gift bags and tissue paper for packaging, or you might need a supply of the gift boxes that you will be using so that you can keep topping up your display as you make sales.

If you're working on your own, you'll need to take some food and drink with you as you might not be able to leave your stall. Once you get used to the fairs you are doing you will know if food is available easily or if you can ask your neighbour to watch things for you. Some organisers don't allow you to eat at your stand – and I wouldn't recommend sitting down to a large meal at any event, but a sandwich and a bottle of water can keep you going through a long day.

Unique Selling Point

Otherwise known as your USP, every business should have a unique selling point, but what is it?

It's what sets you, your business and your designs apart from other people.

It's what your business stands for. It's what's important to you. It is also back to the point of not trying to be everything to everyone.

Working out what your USP is can help you focus your mind on what you actually want to do and how you want to be seen.

Okay, at its simplest, you want to sell your handmade craft.

But why do you want to sell your handcrafted work at all? Is one of your aims to get away from the mass production that we see nowadays? Do you love creating something totally unique, each piece is being a part of your own personality?

Do you want each of your intricate designs to be

a unique work of art? Something collectable and valued as a piece of artwork as much as it is something practical.

Do you concentrate on ethical sourcing of your raw materials, or do you focus on recycling in your design work?

Take some time about your USP. It's a worthwhile process personally as well as for your business. It means that you will be concentrating on why you have started selling your handmade designs.

What do you love about your craft, what do you love about the materials that you use? What are your passions, after all this is not just a job, you have taken the decision to start a creative business of your own, and it's very exciting! If it's not exciting, it might be time to rethink things, because it takes quite a lot of work, and you'll probably find yourself working late into the night sometimes. So it definitely needs to be something that you love doing. And that is the best part about this whole process, being able to make money from something you love doing. It means that you never really go to work!

So think carefully about your USP and then you can design your marketing and the style of your presentation, your shopfront and your packaging around that design concept.

If your UPS is that you upcycle and recycle, you will want that to be reflected in the way you present your designs to the public and your stall will look very different than it would if you design it to show off a range of precious metals and genuine pearl jewellery.

If you work with natural fibres to create children's clothes, make sure that your potential customers know that. If you feel that it's important to work with natural cotton then you want people to know that, and to attract those who feel the same as you do.

If working with the latest fashion colours in your home furnishing designs is your thing – let people know that you're on trend when they look at your stand.

Think about how you want to present yourself and your designs and make sure that everything about your business is telling the same story – from your stand design through to labels, business cards, leaflets and packaging.

Making a Sale

You have chosen your craft, designed and made your product, set your prices, booked your craft fair and set up your stall. Now what?

You have to make your sales.

It's not enough simply to be there and hope that your product sells itself - very few items do and if you don't prepare yourself for the actual process of selling you will be letting your whole venture down. Selling is nowhere near as terrifying as some people fear and at a craft fair you will simply be talking to people who have already shown an interest in your product.

In fact, it can be a great confidence booster when complete strangers praise your work!

Prepare beforehand to give the best service you can to your customer.

Make sure that you have enough change easily available - there's nothing worse than scrabbling around in your pockets or bag looking for coins, even worse if you have to ask a neighbouring stallholder.

Make sure that you look smart - but at the same time take some trouble to make sure that you will be comfortable. Standing all day behind your stand can be awful in uncomfortable shoes, and marquees can be very draughty and bitterly cold especially in November and December. I find it's best to use layering, wear a jacket, cardigan or jumper that you can take off if it does get warmer. For the Christmas markets you'll probably all three plus a hat! Now's the time for that Santa Hat!

If you're going to be on your own, take a drink and something to eat so that you do not have to leave the stand, but try not to make it look like you have set up a picnic!

Price everything clearly. People like to know how much something is before they get sucked into asking questions and being pressurised. Not marking your prices can simply scare customers off, making them assume that if it isn't priced it must be expensive.

Again, this is especially true for Christmas fairs when people are often buying to a price

Have your bags or boxes easily accessible - you don't want to go disappearing under the stand for five minutes while you search around for your packaging.

Have something printed about yourself that makes you look more businesslike, you should want your customers to be able to find you so that they can make further purchases.

If you have a number of fairs booked, print a leaflet with a list of the dates and events where you can be found. Customers like to be able to follow you from fair to fair and having a list that they can keep makes it easy for them to find you at the next event. Many of my regular customers visit fairs because I have put them on my diary leaflet, and many of them do not buy on-line even though they have the details – a great number of people still like to be able to feel and see the gifts they are buying.

If it is appropriate to your product, think about having a simple brochure or leaflet produced so that they can make further orders. Or have business cards available giving your telephone number or address to help your customer to buy from you again – some DO buy on-line!

When a potential customer does approach your stand, you have to look approachable.

Do not hide yourself behind your display as if you don't want to be disturbed.

Do not slump and look fed up - even if you are.

Do not be engrossed in a conversation with your friend or neighbouring stallholder.

Try to look interested in them - without looking too desperate to shake their money out of them.

Smile to let them know that you have seen them, let them look without leaping up to hover over them – that's why it's better to stand than sit behind your stall – leaning forward slightly is much less intimidating than actually standing up.

If someone is taking more than a passing interest, that is the time to involve yourself in conversation. Point out something about your product. If it reflects the light- lift it up to show them, if it has some movement - demonstrate it.

Find something that works for your product, something that gives you an excuse to pick it up and involve the customer. Once you have formed this initial connection it becomes much easier to convert interest into a sale.

Be open when they ask you questions, be interested in them, make parting with their money a pleasure - if it's not, why should they part with it?

Think about how you would like to be treated if you were considering buying yourself a treat

Setting your stall

There is no one best way of setting out your stand. No matter how many fairs and events you have done, each one is slightly different, and although you'll develop a general layout for your stand, don't let it get too set in concrete.

Different rooms will create a different flow of people – sometimes they will approach you from the left, sometimes from the right. I like to set my show stopper pieces at the far end of my stand as they approach. I find that this will stop them and then they look back along the rest of the stand, but if I put it at the beginning, they have walked past before they notice. People are normally looking at eye level and slightly ahead.

I also place the small impulse buy items flat on the table and starting close to the first point they reach, because I find that once a browser notices the stand they will then look down – it means they don't have to make eye contact if they find they're not interested in your items!

So I adapt my display to the space that I find myself in at different fairs, and if things aren't working as well as I'd like, I'll reorganise the display.

Selling is a very important part of the business process. You cannot assume that your work is so good it will just sell itself. Some of it will, but you are in competition for the pound or dollar in the customers pocket and you must work for it.

Don't pounce on anyone who pauses at your stand, you will frighten them off. But don't simply ignore them either. Smile. Say hello, show them that you are actually interested rather than just bored!

You should understand your product – after all you designed and made it! So be prepared to explain it if a potential customer asks questions. Even if you feel that they are simply wasting your time, the fact that you are answering questions, explaining your design, showing how it works, will attract other people who also wanted to know but didn't like to ask – and they might buy from you.

Finishing off the sale in style

Once you have interested them enough to make a sale, package your product attractively. Invest in smart bags and tissue paper rather than newspaper or old supermarket carriers!

The packaging you use depends on your

product. You might be able to use boxes and ribbon to make your hand painted china look even more special, or you could use small gift bags for smaller items. Do remember that packaging matters - that's why we buy designer perfume! Even simple packaging has a purpose – it reflects the image you are trying to create.

The very process of packaging can make the item seem even more special and precious.

Have your tissue paper, ribbons and gift bags within easy reach – you can set up a small table behind your stall for packaging. Think about how they wrap things in the department store for Christmas. 'Would you like it Gift Wrapped?' and then they proceed to make an event out of the wrapping, making a bottle of perfume seem much more special. Certainly more special than simply stuffing it into a carrier bag! And it attracts further sales from those looking on.

Finally, make sure that people can find you again to make more purchases. Put your name or trading title on the product. Have a gift card to slip into the packaging, have a gift tag that you can attach to all your items. Find some way that you can add your name and contact details to every single thing that you sell.

Have cards printed with your details or produce a list of craft fairs that you can be found at in the future and place them on the counter where people can pick them up as they pass.

The power of the impulse purchase
– many pennies make the pounds.

When you are designing your product range it can be very tempting to concentrate on more expensive items, the pieces that really show your skill and ignore the smaller, cheaper ones, but this is a mistake.

Of course it's always very nice to sell something expensive – and you should certainly try to have some special and expensive pieces in your range, they are the designs that will attract the attention in the first place, but many of your sales will be at the smaller end of the scale.

In recessions, the big fashion houses find that lipsticks and nail varnishes sell really well.

Why?

Why would you spend £25 on a lipstick if money is tight?

It's because you might not be able to afford a new designer outfit or bag – but you can still give yourself a treat with a designer lipstick!

So don't ignore the power of the impulse buy.

It's tempting to think that the real profit is in the expensive item on your stall but often the opposite is true. The star of the show might well be the crowd puller - and on that basis alone it will have earned its keep - but at the end of the day when you check your records you will probably find that it is the small, low priced, easily packaged item that has made the real money.

Pocket money purchases, the gifts for colleagues, the teachers at school, the Secret Santa, the stocking fillers and the small extra gift in case you've forgotten someone!

These are the type of sales that really add up and you will almost certainly find that this is where the real profit lies.

If your range is based on higher value products it is probably going to be worth your while to give some thought to how you can adapt your craft to the small impulse purchase. After all, the designer accessories are much better sellers than the couture suits, even for the likes of Chanel and Christian Dior. As always - learn from the experts.

Of course, if you are going to charge less, you must remember to make sure that it also cost you less to make.

Work out how you can increase the speed you can make them at. Will you save time by doing each stage on a number of items at a time rather than working on each one individually from start to finish, think of it as a mini production line.

Not everyone goes to a fair intending or able to buy a wrought iron table, but many more could be tempted by a candle holder, especially with a lovely red Christmas candle with holly wrapped around it – perfect as a Christmas centre piece.

Making Valuable Contacts

While you are at a craft event it is important to realise that there may be other sales opportunities available to you as well as an immediate sale on the day. With some crafts it is as important to make contacts as it is to find an immediate sale.

Every time you set up your stand at a craft fair you are putting your product in front of the general public and you should take every advantage of that.

Of course, the main object of being at a craft fair is to sell your product to those people on that day and to go home with some money, but it's not the only object. You should also be prepared to receive requests for special orders, from someone with a shop who wants to stock your product and even a contract for a larger event.

Think about your product in a wider context and try to see if it has potential for gaining you a larger order for the holiday season.

Many people and businesses will decorate their homes or premises for Christmas, so if you create displays of dried flowers, produce some designs that would be perfect for a beauty salon, small hotel or restaurant, or someone may ask you for a number of arrangements in a special colour for a Christmas party or winter wedding

Safe and interesting toys could be exactly the thing for a kindergarten wanting to give Christmas gifts or handmade body lotions or soaps might be just perfect for a retirement home

If you think that your product does have wider potential, it is probably worth spending some time on doing some initial research and possible even promoting the idea to potential customers.

Christmas Crafts

As I said at the very beginning, there is a difference between selling Christmas crafts and selling crafts at Christmas!

In fact there's a very big difference.

If you're selling your crafts for Christmas you can keep on with the same designs as you sell all year, just adapting them to the Christmas gift season, but if you are selling Christmas crafts then you have to make the holiday season work for you – because that's all you have.

Christmas crafts are items that people will really only buy for the holiday season.

There are some shops that can specialise in the holiday season all year round but they are few and far between and they have to almost create themselves as special shopping destinations to be able to succeed.

You might specialise in tree decorations,

wreaths and swags, other decorations for the mantelpiece, the staircase or the garden.

You could make beautiful nativity scenes, possibly creating heirloom pieces that people will collect year after year, creating their own unique family nativity collection that will be brought out year after year to be put in pride of place for the Christmas celebration.

You may design table pieces, decorations that will make the family meal special with table centres, table linen and Christmas crackers or table gifts.

You could adapt your skills to creating wonderful Christmas cakes and special chutneys, jams or sweets and petit fours.

As a needlewoman you could specialise in creating wonderful Christmas stockings, advent calendars, card holders, napkin holders or Christmas wreaths.

You could design beautiful pieces of handpainted ceramics or glass, elegant candles and candle holders, glittering intricate beadwork stars and angels and of course, beautiful handmade cards, gift boxes and stationary– the list is almost endless as you can see and you can turn almost any craft to Christmas craft, but some things remain the same in all of these items.

They are Christmas crafts.

You will be selling them during the main holiday season and you will be competing with a massive range of other people. Some will be huge department stores selling an enormous range of items to tempt the shopper and charging some very high prices for some of their pieces. At the other end of the scale you will be competing with mass produced items from the Far East sold in markets and in dollar and pound stores – some of them will be on sale in direct competition with you if you do craft and gift fairs or some of the Christmas markets.

So how do you stand out? How will you convince the customer that they should buy from you rather than someone else?

Unless you specialise in high end craft fairs which attract customers who are looking for beautiful handcrafted, unique pieces of work, the sad fact is that most of your customers don't really see the difference between your handmade work and something that is mass produced.

You have to make sure that your work stands out.

Obviously you can do this by creating unique designs that will attract a customer because they want that design rather than they are looking for something handmade. You will also attract some customers who like to be different and don't want the pieces that everybody else can buy in the stores.

Personalisation

But one of the best ways of making your work stand out from the crowd at this very crowded time of the year, is to personalise.

You as a craft worker are in a unique position to

be able to make your work individual to each of your customers.

Make personalisation part of your product range, and make sure that everybody knows this.

You can personalise in many different ways. Often it will involve adding somebody's name to the item. Sewing a child name onto a Christmas stocking, creating sets of Christmas tree baubles, each one personalised for a member of the family. Many types of personalisation can be done on the spot using a range of calligraphy pens or metallic pens, stickers or even having a pre-prepared collection of fabric letters that you can apply as the customer waits.

Think about your craft and the ways in which you could personalise it quickly and easily. People are always very impressed when they watch an artist creating something special, right there in front of them.

You can also personalise the packaging that you put something in adding a name to a gift box or even adding a message on a gift card. Even if calligraphy or fancy writing is not part of your main artwork, practising it so that you feel confident in personalising your designs is well worth doing. Although you can buy many items with the name that have been mass produced, lots of people have unusual names or unusual spelling and being able to buy a personalised item for them is very special.

Special orders

Another type of personalisation is to create designs in your customer's choice of colours. Although you can go a long way towards this with the designs you have already created and have available for sale on the day, you can also offer a service by special order to create a one off design for a client. This could involve producing decorations in an unusual range of colours, coordinating the decorations for the Christmas table to match an existing colour palette in the room or including a particular motif into your design.

Of course these cannot be done on the day, they have to be special orders giving you time to create them.

If you do decide that you would like to create special orders you will have to make some preparations to make this work for you.

Create an order form where you can write down exactly what is required and what has been agreed. You will need to take a deposit if not full payment for the work because if your client doesn't return for the order you will be unlikely to be able to sell it to someone else. If you decide to take a deposit only make sure that it covers the cost of your parts so that you will not be out of pocket completely.

Once you have completed the order form with all the details and your client's contact details go over this with your client and get them to sign the form. Make sure that you both have a copy so that there is no misunderstanding later on.

You will also have to decide how long it will take you to produce these orders. You will have to have a cut-off date which will give you time to create the order, and you will have to keep a diary so that you do not take on too many special orders. Although it is wonderful to take orders for custom work it is also very important to develop a reputation for being reliable which means being able to produce the orders with your normal care and on time.

Arrange a delivery time when you take the order. There is no point assuming that it is required for Christmas Eve if the client actually wants it for a big party a week before that.

Good communication is vital when you are dealing with special orders it is far too easy for both sides to think they know what has been decided while actually being poles apart. That's why it is so important to get everything in writing.

Planning your work

Although you're selling season will be quite short - September to December - that doesn't mean that you are only going to work four months of the year.

You will want to take advantage of every selling opportunity that you can during your short selling season and this can mean that you are working far more than the normal one or two days a week if you do craft fairs at the weekend throughout the year.

You may find that you are working 5, 6 or even 7 days a week throughout some of this period if you do the traditional fairs, Christmas markets, school and church fairs and possibly some house parties. You might find yourself doing two or more events on a single day.

It is great. It means lots of selling opportunities, but the last thing you need is to run out of stock halfway through. You certainly do not want to find yourself either having to cancel events or working late into the night to create more stock. Not only is it very exhausting, your standards will begin to slip as you continually work long hours into the night and your work will not stay at the high quality that you want. And although you might think it would be exciting to sell so much that you need to stay up till 2 o'clock in the morning in fact it will soon begin to pall and you will begin to hate your new business.

So you still need to consider your business as a year round operation, whether you combine it with employment or run it as a full time business. Even if you only intend to do craft fairs at the weekends while you work at your main employment during the week you still want to spend most of the year preparing your stock.

Ideally you should start in January.

There are a number of reasons for this. The obvious one is that gives you plenty of time to create your designs, start planning your displays organising your packaging and then actually making your crafts.

One of the less obvious ones is that you can actually pick up a lot of bargains in January. After all who wants to buy Christmas designs, festive rubberstamps, papers, fabric or plain Christmas tree baubles in January?

If you have the space to store them, this is the ideal time to stock up on your raw materials. You can save a fortune and you will have the parts you need. It can be very difficult to find the right designs in April or May when you want to be making your Christmas crafts.

Storage is another very important part of this type of Christmas business. You need to have the space to store your stock for months and you need to be able to keep it in top condition. Obviously this is not quite so difficult if you are creating small delicate designs but if you intend to create large pieces such as Christmas wreaths you might need a lot more storage space. It also needs to be dry and clean. There is no point spending hours on creating your designs only to find that they are damp and tatty when you come to your Christmas fairs.

I prefer to store my finished pieces in clear plastic boxes with tight fitting lids.

This means that they can stack easily, I can see what is in each box and they will stay dry, clean and safe ready to hit the stall in September looking fresh and pristine even if I actually made the piece in January

Crafts for Christmas

While Christmas crafts are all about the Christmas season, there are many other crafts that can be sold all year but that can be adapted or packaged to appeal to people who are searching for Christmas gifts.

If you choose this model for your craft business it means that you are not restricted to the main holiday season selling period.

You can sell your crafts all year round, taking advantage of all the different promotional opportunities during the year, such as Valentine's Day, Easter, Mother's Day, Father's Day, birthdays, summer holidays, weddings, anniversaries, Chinese New Year, new babies, Thanksgiving, Independence Day and anything else you can think of!

But you should still pay special attention to the Christmas season. After all it is one of the main marketing seasons of the year for almost any retail business.

Alternatively you can organise your business so that you still concentrate on the main Christmas season, choosing fairs, markets and events that fall in the September to December period.

In this way you can spend most of the year preparing your stock, but concentrating your selling on the festive season. This does suit some craftworkers who prefer not to be out at fairs throughout the whole year, but to concentrate their bookings into a shorter season. It means that you can have the summer period free for other activities or you can focus your attention on other parts of your life such as a full time career, family and actually having a life! If you do work full time it can be very difficult to also work at craft fairs at the weekends and still have time to actually make your crafts never mind eating and sleeping and generally having a life!

So focusing your selling on the Christmas season, when you have the best chance of making more sales, does make sense for a lot of people.

Seasonal Designs

Christmas is the time for special festive designs and they can be worked into almost any craft. Reindeer on ceramics, snowmen on candle holders, Christmas trees on notepads and Santas on baby's bibs.

Almost any craft can be adapted to the Christmas theme.

Take a look in the stores to see how many items

can be decorated with snowflakes, Christmas puddings, candy canes, cheerful robins and winter sleighs.

You can certainly get carried away with your ideas, but do remember that not everyone wants to wear Christmas trees in their ears or go around wearing festive jumpers all the time.

You should always offer some of your work in designs that are not restricted to the Christmas theme, so that you are not restricting your sales too much.

Another important thing to remember when you're planning your stock is that if you concentrate on Festive themes, you will be left with any items that haven't sold by Christmas Eve, not many people want to buy a beautiful snowflake table runner in January.

This means that you will have to store all the items you have left very carefully until the following September when the whole party kicks off again.

If you find yourself reaching the end of your list of events and you still have a quite a lot of some of your festive designs, you might want to consider putting them on special offer so that you are not left with too much stock at the end of the year.

Creating Gifts

Of course you can decide than you are not going to change your actual designs for the Christmas season if you sell throughout the year or even if you do focus your event in the holiday season. But even if you're not going to actually create Christmas designs, the way you present them should be different from the rest of the year.

For instance, if you are a jeweller you could decide to make designs featuring beads of rich reds and greens, or earrings with snowflakes or snowmen but you might decide to simply to stay with your trademark designs, working with the colours and gems that you use all year. But even if your designs don't change the way you package them should.

When you were doing your market research you would have noticed that, although the products inside the gift packaging are often quite ordinary and available all year round, the way they are presented turns them into a Christmas gift.

So if you are a jeweller, you should create sets of designs rather than selling earrings and pendants separately. Make it easy for the potential customer to see your item as a gift. Although you might have the earrings and the pendants sitting alongside one another on your display, once you present them both in a single gift box they become a set and that turns them into a Christmas present.

The same can be said of almost any craft. If you create beautiful hand-painted ceramics, package your bone China mug with some luxury chocolates, wrapping it up in cellophane and tying a beautiful ribbon around the top. Or you could create a gift box with your hand painted China sitting alongside some shortbread or a box of high quality teabags.

Spend some time thinking about how you can

turn your particular craft into a ready-made gift that can compete for the customers spending with the gifts that are available in the department stores and large chains.

Although you don't have to start this type of planning in January you do have to start quite early in the year, certainly by midyear, to make sure that you have everything in place.

You need to give yourself time to design your packaging and time to source the boxes, ribbons or papers that you will need.

Planning and preparation is very important in creating ready-made gifts for the holiday season. If you leave it too late you will simply run out of time and you won't make the most of your selling opportunities. Although you might not rely on the Christmas season for your business nobody wants to turn down additional sales and income that can come with this very important retail season.

So set aside time to look at your product range and to see it as a gift on a department store shelf. What kind of boxes could you use, where will you source them, how much will they cost – the cost has to be built into the price you will charge. How will you set your items in the box? Can you use shredded tissue paper? Will you have to design and make an insert? Can you use clear cellophane and beautiful ribbon instead – you can often source them from a floristry supplies company.

You should do this work, design your packaging and arrange where you can get the supplies you will need long before the actual festive season. You should really have done all the planning by midsummer, so that you will know what you can offer and how much you will charge for your seasonal gift range by the time you start the festive fair season in September.

Personalisation

Personalisation can also bring in many extra sales even if your designs aren't specifically Christmas related. Even a simple notepad is suddenly much more special if the recipients name has been added to the cover.

Plain wooden objects such as hairbrushes, keyholders, a desk tidy or key ring can become special personalised gifts with the art of pyrography, you can even create unique house signs with the name or number of the house on a wooden plaque.

Think of how you can add personalisation to your craft and let people know that it is a service that you offer.

People are often looked frantically looking for something different at Christmas and of course this is where the craft artist is perfectly positioned to take advantage of the holiday panic.

Whatever your work is, it is different.

It is not available in the mass-market - or at least it shouldn't be!

If you are handcrafting your designs there is no point in simply copying what is available in the main market. You will not be able to compete on quantity or price. You are limited to how many pieces you can make - after all you are not factory - and you shouldn't be trying to compete on price. Your items should be exclusive not cheap. Good value for money is wonderful and will attract customers, cheap will just make your beautiful work look second-rate, and rather than attracting customers it will actually put people off. After all, who wants to buy a cheap Christmas present?

One of the biggest advantages of selling your handcrafted designs as Christmas presents is that your customer can be sure that their gift is not going to be replicated.

If they buy a CD, a scarf and hat set, some beautiful bath foam and body lotion or a piece of jewellery from the large department store or chain store, someone else could give exactly the same gift, especially if it specifically suits the person it has been bought for.

When they buy a gift from you it is extremely unlikely that the gift will be duplicated. After all that would mean that two people had to purchase exactly the same things from you, for exactly the same person and the odds against that have got to be high!

Make sure that your customers realise this. You'd be amazed at how many people do not realise that you make everything yourself, even when you're in a craft fair, and of course this is a much bigger problem if you're selling at Christmas markets or other events.

I've lost track of how many people have looked at me in surprise and said "you make this yourself?"

So don't assume that people will realise that it's all your own work, make signs for your table, include it in your packaging and make it obvious as you speak to people. For instance you could let them know that you could make the piece in a different colour for them, or in a different size, or that you've only ever made ten pieces in that design.

This is a very important part of your marketing plan, because the fact that you create your own designs, that your work is handmade and that it can't simply be bought in any outlet store, is one of your main selling points.

Your work genuinely is a designer gift, bought directly from the actual designer. The word 'designer' has been totally overused in recent years to describe everything from household linen to cosmetics and kitchen equipment, all of which is mass produced.

So make the most of the fact that a gift bought from you is a genuine designer piece.

Special offer marketing

More than any other, this is the time of year where price matters.

Your customers have a huge list of things that they have to spend their money on for Christmas and budgeting has become more and more important in recent years when people are choosing not to build up large credit card bills that have to be cleared in the New Year.

There are so many things that have to come out of the Christmas budget, decorations, food, travel, Christmas parties and of course Christmas gifts both large and small.

Price points

So your customers will have a price point in mind as they look for each gift on their list and you should hit these prices in your display. £5, £10, £15, £20 (or $'s). Check the displays of gifts in your local department stores to see how they do this.

Hitting the right price points makes it easier for your customer to tick the required presents off the Christmas shopping list, and making it easy for the customer is one of the best ways of making sales at this time of the year.

After all, time is at a premium as well as money, so if you can make it easy for someone to buy the gifts they are looking for at the price they want to pay, they are much more likely to buy them from you.

The other benefit is that once someone stops at your stand and can see that they can solve some of their shopping easily, they will probably look around the rest of your selection and choose more of your gifts from different price ranges to tick off more of their shopping list.

Special offers

You could decide to take an even bigger piece of marketing theory from the department stores and use some of their promotional marketing techniques.

'Three for Two.'

'£5 each – 5 for £20.'

'£6 each - Two for £10'

The most popular offer is '3 for 2' - of course, when you are adding up the total cost of their shopping, do remember that it's always the lowest priced item that is free!

This is another time you should learn from the experts.

They have found that - particularly during the Christmas season - this promotion will encourage people to buy two items, in order to get the third one free, rather than just the one item that they actually went in for. In fact, you can find yourself spending ages in front of the shelves wondering who you will give the extra two gifts to, and what you should choose, when it would be much quicker and cheaper to just pick the one you wanted in the first place. But that's the point. It works. And if the big stores can make the most of it - so can you.

Of course, do remember that they are all priced to cover the cost of the three items, even though as a shopper you feel that you are getting a bargain, and there's that wonderful magic word – FREE!

So if you decide to use this promotion, do make sure that you work out your prices correctly. You're not actually in the business of giving away your designs – even at Christmas!

Unique gifts

As a crafter you are in the perfect position to offer your customers that magical mix of a unique gift that cannot be priced easily by the person who receives it.

Your customers can find the perfect gift for almost anybody and it will be unique. Whoever they give it to won't be able to go to the January sales and see how much they spent! And they don't have to worry about someone else giving exactly the same gift - a problem you do have to consider when you choose a book or DVD!

All styles of craft can be adapted for the Christmas gift market, so make the most of it. It can mean that the Christmas season is your most profitable time of the year.

If you have spent the time and thought to create Christmas gifts and to present them to your customer as Christmas gifts you will have much more success in selling them as Christmas gifts.

Even if you decide that your designs can't be packaged into ready box to presents, think about how else you can add to the Christmas theme to your products. Find some way to make it easy for the customer to choose, purchase and walk away with the Christmas presents she needs.

If you can go that extra step and send her away with them beautifully wrapped, ribboned and ready to set under the Christmas tree – job done - You'll have saved them time as well as the extra cost of gift wrapping.

The other side of Christmas

And no – I don't mean the January sales!

The problem with Christmas is that the shops are full of Christmas stuff!

That's wonderful if you're looking for Christmas presents, cards and decorations but an absolute nightmare if you're looking for cards and presents for birthdays, anniversaries or any other event that's not Christmas. And I say this as someone who has a number of family birthdays and anniversaries that fall in the October – January slot.

There are many opportunities to profit from this gap in the market. For instance, if you sell handmade cards you are in an ideal situation to solve this problem for your customers. The card shops are stuffed full of Christmas cards from about September, with all other events crushed into a corner at the back of the shop, so if you want a card for a birthday in December you have to either be really well organised and buy it in July or make do with the tiny choice you have in December.

It can be so tempting to pack your stall with every imaginable design of Christmas card, but don't. You can certainly have a selection of beautiful, exclusive Christmas card designs, but you're never going to be able to compete with the millions of cards on sale in every store and from every charity you can think of.

But if you have a good selection of birthday, anniversary, good luck, congratulation, new baby, new house, wedding, engagement, sympathy, and cards for every other event you can think of you will be able to fill the huge gap left by everyone else.

And it doesn't finish at Christmas. Any time of the year that is dominated by a special holiday can make it difficult to buy anything not directly associated with that holiday.

Valentine's Day, Mother's Day, Easter and Halloween will see the stores swamped with seasonal designs. So although they are a good source of seasonal sales, don't forget the potential customers who are looking for something else.

Although handmade cards are an obvious craft for the 'Christmas' affect almost any crafter can take advantage of this gap in the market.

So you should take this into account when you are creating your beautifully packaged gift boxes.

Make some of them more general rather than all Christmas. When a customer is looking for a gift for a birthday in December, they don't want it to look like a Christmas present, they want a birthday present and it can be almost impossible to find a gift that doesn't look as if it belongs under the Christmas tree

The job of any retailer is to supply what the customer wants, so if they want a birthday, anniversary or engagement gift, make sure that you can offer something that will fit the bill.

Business Promotion

Promoting your business

You should always promote your business.

You want to be able to create customer loyalty, to attract people back to your business time after time. After all if they like what you're selling you want them to buy again.

There are all types of promotions that are designed to encourage customer loyalty. They should also create the style of your brand, and remind potential customers about you and of course they should increase sales.

The main chance to promote your craft business is at the point-of-sale, at a craft fair, the Christmas market or any other events that you are at.

Have a supply of business cards or leaflets about your business on the table so that it is easy to pick up even if that person is not purchasing from you on the day.

If you are doing a season of events, produce a leaflet of all the dates and event details. This means that someone can look at your designs, pick up a date leaflet, go away and think about it deciding who your designs would be suitable for, and then they will know where to find you the following week or the following month.

Many people like to have the chance to think about items before they actually make a purchase. This is easy if they are looking in the stores, they can always go back the next day or the next week. You need to make it easy for them to come to you because they can't simply return to the same shop when you are not a shop.

Of course you should continue to promote your business to people who do actually make a purchase. If you have a date leaflet put a copy in with every purchase. If you have a website put a card in the packaging that promotes that site. If you do house parties, produce a leaflet that explains about that.

You also want to make sure that everyone who has a piece of your work knows that it is your unique craft and design, even if they haven't actually purchased it but have received it as a gift. This means that they will be able to buy more items from you either for themselves or when they want to give a gift.

Christmas is the perfect opportunity to expand your customer base.

People who would never visit a crafts fair will have the opportunity to experience your work, so make sure that they know how to find you when they want to buy some more directly from you.

Some events, especially charity events, ask you to provide a gift for their raffle -and of course you want to support the charity - but make sure that whoever wins your piece knows where it's from. There's nothing wrong with supporting your business as well as the charity.

Every piece of work that leaves your stall should be branded in some way.

The way you add your logo will depend on the style of your craft but don't think that it has to be something expensively produced by a professional printer. The beauty of your craft is that it is individually handmade, so there's nothing wrong with your packaging being handmade as well. In fact it adds to your overall style.

If you make chunky vintage style jewellery, why not find some manila luggage tags and write your details by hand on them. If your work is in delicate handpainted silk, create a delicate leaflet to put in the box with it.

Again, learn from the experts. Visit the stores and actually 'look' at the packaging. It's very easy to take things for granted. We're so used to being surrounded by products that sometimes we don't really look anymore.

Have a proper look at the products on offer in your range – whether that's jewellery, handmade quilts, ceramics, woodwork, home decor – whatever you feel is in the same type of product range. Then look at the different styles and price ranges. They will all be presented in different ways – but they'll all have the maker's details on them somewhere.

Find a style you like and that you feel will complement your designs and work from there to create your own unique packaging and labelling.

Packaging the packaging

Your packaging and presentation doesn't stop with the design of your box, pouch or other container.

Think about how you are going to hand it over. After all, you not just going to hand somebody a box or packet. You will want to put it in an outer bag, possibly a small gift bag, and you must always include some form of business card. It could be a simple business card with your name or business name, your logo and contact details. Or it could be a special romance card giving some information about you, how you design your pieces, what your inspiration is, or details about the specific piece of work they have bought.

I have a friend at craft shows who puts all her items in little boxes. The boxes are very nice, but the finishing touch is the fact that she ties them all with beautiful ribbon. It takes a little bit of extra time, and it makes every customer feel that she is putting a little bit of extra effort into their purchase. People don't mind waiting, they don't even mind waiting while she finishes packing someone else's order. She has lots of repeat customers!

And of course the packaging can be an advert in itself.

If you put your designs into a lovely little gift bag, which just so happens to have your logo hanging on a tag from the bag handle, then every one of your customers will be advertising you as they walk around the rest of the event. Just another little marketing idea you can liberate from the large stores and designer companies!

Choose your packaging to suit your image. There's a huge range of packaging available. You might choose natural jute or hemp bags to suit your designs if you work with the natural wooden beads or recycled materials.

Small brown paper bags might be exactly the kind of look you want if you create designs out of natural materials.

Glamorous scarf designs might call for elegant black and gold bags, while delicate silver jewellery designs might look perfect in silver hologram gift bags.

You could even buy plain craft bags and design the whole look yourself, even having a rubberstamp made of your logo and printing the bags yourself.

Christmas is a perfect time for finding a beautiful range of gift bags to suit any style. Bright and funky, cool and elegant, vintage, retro – almost any style is available nowadays – just make sure you source your packaging in time, it can take a while to arrive if you choose to buy in bulk from the Far East.

Talking about your craft.

One of the nice things about selling face-to-face is the fact that you actually get a chance to meet your customers. So make the most of it.

If you sell jewellery you have to be aware that they could buy a piece of jewellery anywhere - at any of the other stalls at the fair, at any fashion shop, jewellery shop or even supermarket. But they want to buy the jewellery from you. So talk to them about it.

The same is true whatever your craft. Handmade cards and papercraft or large pieces of handcarved wooden furniture. Your pieces are unique to you and you should make sure that your customers know that they are talking to a craft worker who loves their work. Even at a craft fair some customers don't seem to realise that you actually make everything you offer for sale.

When you look around at many events, you will always find some designers who just sit behind their stall, often reading a book. Put yourself in the position of the potential customer. If you were thinking of buying something from that stall, you'd probably just walk past.

Why should you show interest in their work if they can't show interest in you?

You also have to remember that a lot of people would feel uncomfortable about disturbing someone who has obviously got something better to do than to talk to them.

So, stand behind or to the side of your stall. Smile at people, engage with them, say hello.

You don't have to pounce on every potential customer, that is counter-productive, but you should show them that you are aware that they are standing in front of your stall and that you are willing to talk to them if they would like to ask a question.

When you do open a conversation, talk about your craft. What makes it different? What is your USP (unique selling point). After all, you now know what your style is, so you should also know why your designs are different to anyone else's.

Do you always include a piece of Jade in your jewellery designs, because it is the gem of health, wealth and long life?

Are your designs made from pieces of polished glass that you personally collect from the beach?

Is recycling an important aspect of your work?

Can you personalise any of the items on your stand while that wait?

What led you into your craft, what is your story?

Tell them that you can customise pieces, changing the colours of the fabrics, altering the length of a bracelet or personalising your design. Taking orders for bespoke pieces can be a very valuable addition to your craft business.

When somebody does buy a piece, point out - without pressure – other items in your range that are designed to make a set.

And don't be afraid to talk to someone, even though you have a strong feeling that they are not going to buy anything from you - at least today. They may well come back on another day when they do want to buy a piece, and they will remember that you were friendly and didn't pressurise them.

Or you might sell to the people who were listening to your conversation - lots of people prefer to join a crowd when they wouldn't approach you themselves.

It also creates a good impression if anyone is looking around for craft workers to take a stall at their event or give a talk to their group. They will be looking for people who are open and approachable.

A final word

The Business of Business

This book is all about marketing and selling your handmade designs, it is not about the legal, financial and tax requirements of running a business – any business of any size.

Find some expert advice

There are many books and courses and websites available where you can find out about these other areas of running your business and I recommend that you invest some time and money in this information so that you can avoid any pitfalls and problems in the future.

www.ingramcontent.com/pod-product-compliance
Lightning Source LLC
Chambersburg PA
CBHW051332170526
45166CB00002B/789